Health and My Body

Food Is Fuel

by Mari Schuh

PEBBLE
a capstone imprint

Pebble Explore is published by Pebble, an imprint of Capstone.
1710 Roe Crest Drive
North Mankato, Minnesota 56003
www.capstonepub.com

Library of Congress Cataloging-in-Publication Data is available on the Library of Congress website.
ISBN: 978-1-9771-2386-2 (library binding)
ISBN: 978-1-9771-2686-3 (paperback)
ISBN: 978-1-9771-2423-4 (eBook PDF)

Summary: We need food to keep our bodies going. But what are healthy foods and why should we eat them? Learn how to make healthy food choices.

Image Credits
iStockphoto: Hispanolistic, 23, kali9, 27, paulaphoto, 15, shapecharge, 10, skynesher, 22, Wavebreakmedia, 9; Shutterstock: AlexeiLogvinovich, 16, ANURAK PONGPATIMET, 29, beats1, 19, Brent Hofacker, 11, Darrin Henry, 6, Dragon Images, 24, Hafizussalam bin Sulaiman, 14, Kdonmuang, 25, KPG Payless2, 17, leonori, 8, Monkey Business Images, Cover, 5, 21, photonova, design element, Prostock-studio, 13, Vladislav Noseek, 12, Yulia Davidovich, 7

Editorial Credits
Editor: Michelle Parkin; Designer: Sarah Bennett; Media Researcher: Morgan Walters; Production Specialist: Laura Manthe

Printed in the United States 5595

Table of Contents

Bold words are in the glossary.

Healthy Foods

Think of all the food you ate today. Did you eat a big breakfast or a bowl of cereal? Did you have some fruit with your lunch? What did you eat for dinner?

The food you eat is fuel for your body. Some food gives you **energy**. Others slow you down. Healthy food makes your body go. You can learn and play!

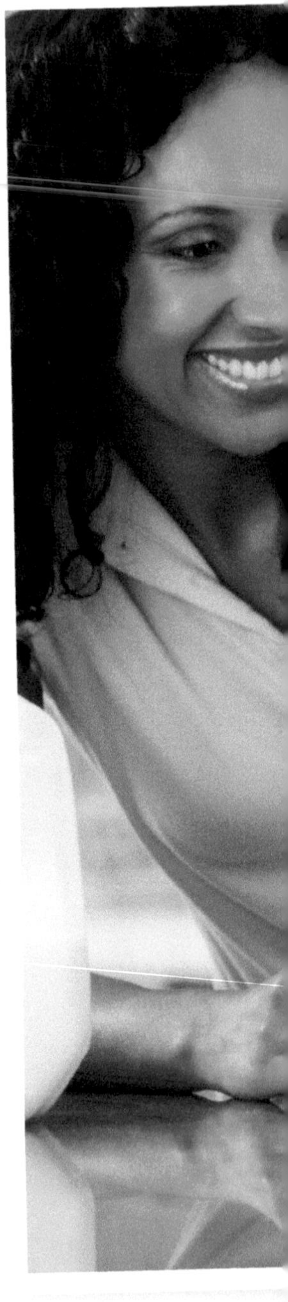

Eating healthy food keeps you strong. It keeps you healthy and happy. Healthy food helps your body and mind. It helps you grow. It keeps you **alert** in school.

Food gives your body **nutrients**. Your body needs nutrients to stay healthy. Nutrients can help your body heal when you are sick. What food is good for your body and brain? Let's find out!

Fruits and Vegetables

At mealtimes, half of your plate should be filled with fruits and vegetables. You should eat 1 to 1½ cups of fruit a day. Fruits have nutrients that your body needs.

You can eat fresh fruit. Canned fruit is healthy too, as long as it's in water or 100 percent juice. Dried and frozen fruit are good for you. Eat fruit whole or cut up. Put fruit in a smoothie.

Vegetables are an important part of a healthy **diet**. Try to eat 1½ to 2½ cups of veggies each day. You can eat fresh, frozen, or canned veggies. Snack on celery or tomatoes. Cook and mash up a sweet potato. Dunk raw veggies into dip.

Vegetables have **vitamins** to keep you healthy. Carrots have vitamin A. This helps your skin and eyes. Broccoli has vitamin C for healthy teeth.

Grains, Dairy, and Protein

Grains help fuel your body. Cereal and pasta are grains. Food made from rice and wheat are also grains. Bread and oatmeal are in this food group too.

Try to eat whole grains, such as brown rice and whole wheat bread. They have more nutrients. Ask a parent to buy whole grain foods for the whole family. Eat brown rice with dinner. Chomp on whole wheat crackers with cheese. Munch on some popcorn.

Milk and cheese are dairy foods. Yogurt is too. Dairy foods have vitamin D and **calcium**. Calcium builds strong bones and teeth.

Eat some yogurt as a snack. Low-fat cottage cheese and fruit are good too. Look for dairy foods that are low in fat. Have an adult make you a smoothie with fruit and low-fat yogurt.

Your body needs **protein** to grow. Food with protein helps build strong bones and muscles.

Meat, chicken, and fish all have protein. Eat eggs for a healthy breakfast. Enjoy tuna at lunch. Nuts and seeds have protein too. Spread some peanut butter on whole grain toast. Eat a small bowl of chili for dinner.

Unhealthy Foods

Not all food is good for you. Candy, cakes, and other sweet treats are full of sugar. Soda, chips, and deep-fried foods are not healthy either. This type of food is called junk food. It might give you a burst of energy, but it does not last long. Then you'll feel tired and run down.

It is OK to have some junk food once in a while. You can enjoy it in small amounts. Eat it as a treat.

Eating Well

When it comes to food, it's important to listen to your body. Are you hungry or just bored? Eat when you feel hungry.

During mealtimes, sit at the dinner table. Put away your cell phone. Turn off the TV. Pay attention to what you are eating. Eat slowly and enjoy your food. It'll be easier to listen to what your body is telling you. Stop eating when you feel full. It's OK to leave food on your plate.

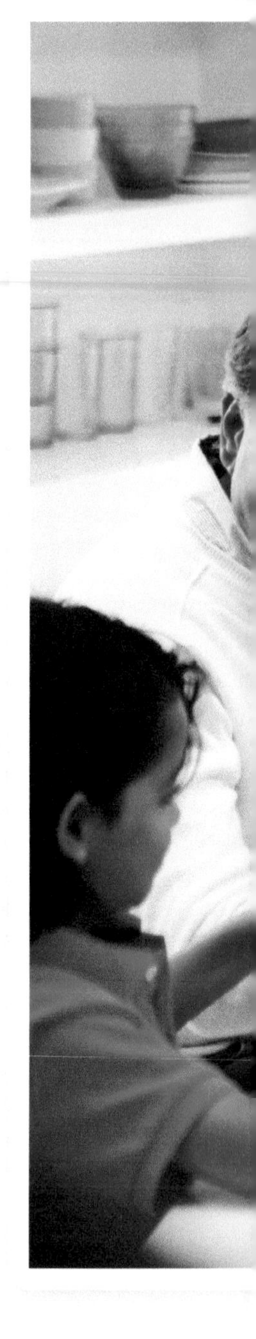

Are you ready to eat healthy? Set some food goals. How many new, healthy foods will you try this week? How many vegetables will you eat each day? Write down your goals in a journal or notebook. Keep track of how you do during the week.

Plan ahead. Go food shopping with a family member. Help make a grocery list. Think of healthy foods that you like to eat. You could also visit a farmer's market. You might find some new foods to try!

You can help make meals at home. Take the food out of the refrigerator. Wash fruits and veggies. Rip up lettuce for a salad. Set the table. Enjoy eating with your family or friends. After the meal, help clean up. Wash the dishes. Put away everything.

Start a vegetable garden. Ask a parent if you can make a vegetable garden at home. Choose the vegetable seeds. A parent can help you plant them. Water the seeds and watch them grow.

No vegetable garden at home? No problem! Look for **community** gardens nearby. You and a parent can help grow vegetables there. You could also meet people in your community who enjoy healthy eating.

24

Healthy eating is a big part of a healthy life. It's important to eat a variety of healthy food. Be sure to eat fruits, dairy, vegetables, protein, and whole grains each day. Fill your plate with colorful food!

Eating well will help you be smart and strong. You will have energy to play and have fun!

Glossary

alert (uh-LURT)—awake and paying attention

calcium (KAL-see-uhm)—a mineral needed for strong teeth and bones

community (kuh-MYOO-nuh-tee)—a group of people who live in the same area

diet (DY-uht)—the kinds of food a person eats on a regular basis

energy (E-nuhr-jee)—the ability to do work, such as move things

nutrient (NOO-tree-uhnt)—a part of food, such as a vitamin, that is used for growth

protein (PROH-teen)—a substance found in foods such as meat, milk, eggs, and beans that is an important part of a person's diet

vitamin (VYE-tuh-min)—a nutrient that helps keep people healthy

Read More

Clark, Rosalyn. *Why We Eat Healthy Foods.* Minneapolis: Lerner Publications, 2018.

Marsico, Katie. *Eat Healthy Foods!* Ann Arbor, MI: Cherry Lake Publishing, 2019.

Mason, David I.A. *Healthy Foods Make Your Body Go.* Minneapolis: Cantata Learning, 2016.

Internet Sites

Go, Slow, and Whoa! A Kid's Guide to Eating Right
https://kidshealth.org/en/kids/go-slow-whoa.html

MyPlate Kids' Place
https://www.choosemyplate.gov/browse-by-audience/view-all-audiences/children/kids

PBS Kids: Nutrition
https://pbskids.org/arthur/health/nutrition/

Index